The Spirit of Nature

ABBY PENNINGTON

Copyright © 2019 Abby Pennington

All rights reserved. No part of this publication may be reproduced, distributed, or transmitted in any form or by any means, including photocopying, recording, or other electronic or mechanical methods, without the prior written permission of the publisher, except in the case of brief quotations embodied in critical reviews and certain other noncommercial uses permitted by copyright law.

Contact the author at the following:
Email: apennington007@gmail.com
Instagram: spiritofnaturepoet & abbygpennington

Book and graphic design by Carl Pennington, 212films.com
Edited by Abigail Grace Pennington

First Printing, 2019
ISBN 978-1-64204-331-0

Printed in the United States of America

To those who aren't afraid to swim in the depths of life

The Spirit of Nature

Poetry by Abby Pennington

Contents

Great Outdoors /6

Love Charms /32

Bold Explorers /88

Mysterious Humans /119

GREAT OUTDOORS

Nature calls
In distant whispers
Smiles of sunlight
Glances of trees
Hugs of wind
Kisses of flowers
Let us escape
Into the wild
Let us be captivated
By the beauty
Of the natural scene
Together we are called
Let us answer

I see
Earth colors
Green and blue
In the wilderness
And suddenly
I become
A curious soul
Who ventures
Down the path
Of unknown
Until I feel
A lasting peace
That refreshes me
With vibrancy
To endlessly roam
And I'm ok
With being lost
And never found

Look at the sky
Ought it be an example
The clouds pass by
Never going back
The sun shines
After a harsh storm
The snow falls
Decorating the ground
The rain pours
Flourishing the earth
We should too
Let the past go by
Cast rays of joy
Spread blankets of love
Release torrents of hope
Never letting a dreary day
Bring us to gloom
Or overcast our skies
We are our own sky
Choose to see beauty
In any weather
With a positive mind

Ocean breeze
Sing me a song
Bright sun
Rest my heart
Free birds
Lift my spirit
To be
Barefoot and careless
A little reckless
Water dweller
Surfing the waves
Until the days
Are gone
And time
Is carried away
By the sea

Elements of silence
Peace within the soul
Kaleidoscope of dreams
In the mystic morning
Harmonious sounds of nature
Awake the euphoric senses
To the lush vast earth
The serene cerulean sky
Send a caressing wind
Sing melodious lullabies
And tender beams of sunlight
Swathe layers of warmth
Around the essence
Of a yugen spirit

Grow strong
Like the mountains
As you journey
On the path
Of life
Even if you stumble
During a quake
Stand back up
And remember
To reach for
The blue blanket
Of strength
Above you
Aim high

A sunflower
Amidst a field of roses
Seems out of place
A peculiar inhabitant
Compared to the others
A unique individual
That catches stares
Of disapproval
For being different
This odd flower
Is the best kind
For it fearlessly stands
Proud of its identity
While the roses all shrivel
Terrified by the boldness
By the liberty
Of the sunflower
Who never cared it was yellow
When everyone else was red

Plant a seed within me
To sprout indigenous thoughts
In my mind
To form roots
Of authentic creativity
That branch throughout
My entire being
I wish to grow
Under the care
Of Mother Nature
She guides my heart
To treat the earth tenderly
And live differently
Dwelling outdoors
Barefoot in the dirt
Naked in the sunlight
She leads me down
The humble path
That goes against them
The ones who lack respect
For the art of nature
The ones who trash the ground
Who pollute the air
Who harm the oceans
Who destruct the mountains
With careless actions
Who refuse to see
The affectionate splendor
Of Mother Nature
Of savoring the beauty
Of caring for the world
Graciously given
Plant a seed within them
To sprout indigenous thoughts
So they'll see
Nature is treasure
Not for the greed of man

Into the depths
Let the worries
Drown away
Let the salt
Cleanse the mind
A place of revival
In deep blue
Serene current
Caress the soul
To belong
To breathe
To flow
With the sea
To stay
Forever
In paradise

At the arrival
Of grand sunrise
Colors of red and gold
Are paint strokes
Across the sky
As if the sun
Were an artist
Stroking a brush
Over a canvas
To complete
A divine work
So mesmerizing
You can't look away
Until the finish
When the sun
Has fully risen
And the sky beholds
A masterpiece

Beloved waters
Speak to the depths
Of my soul
Stir within this heart
The enchanting song
Of the horizon
At the shifting
Of the tide
Lure me in deeper
With an oceanic embrace
Currents flow through
My veins and bones
Allow the salt
To drown out the sounds
And remove me
From the world above
Movements of energy
Wrap me in
The surging arms
Of the sea
No return to land
Captive to underwater
In this rest
I reach serenity
The world of blue
My pure deliverance

Do you hear the call
The whispers of nature
Trying to save you
To ease your pain
To lift your spirit
By way of naturality
The beautiful raw earth
The incomparable sight
Of sun shining
Trees blowing
Waves crashing
Mountains standing
Snow falling
All for you
To cleanse your soul
To awaken your senses
The proof
The reassurance
That hope is real
As nature is pure

Nature brings healing
Stronger than any medicine
Are the breaths of fresh air
And the streams of sunlight
Provide the greatest vitamin
While the salty sea
Brings upon restoration
There is a cure
To the disease
Outside the confines
Found in the natural haven
This innate remedy
Revives a soul wholly
Renews a spirit fully
As if reborn
From a radical cleanse
All one has to do
Is immerse themselves
In the therapy
Of nature

What if words
Were thought
Before spoken
What if actions
Were analyzed
Before done
Could the world
Ever be a place
Of harmony
Where love and peace
Overflowed the spirit
Instead of hate and war
Where trees were planted
Oceans purely clean
Grass never littered

Hypnotic state
Fully transfixed
On the curvature
Of glorious waves
The sound of energy
Saltwater surging
Moving to meet
The longing shore
To kiss my toes
To ignite my soul
Heal my spirit
Energize my body
With the promise
Of something
Fresh and new
To come my way
I wait hopefully
Like the shore
Awaiting the tide
To shift the waves
And quench
What once was dry

Henceforth the snow
Ceased to fall
After relinquishing
A magical dust
On the arboreous realm
That is now
A mystical wonderland
Of white
A reminder
Of pristine nostalgia
A landmark
Of elemental appeal
For the eyes
To treasure
As sacred
To bask in
The psychic occurrence
In satisfaction
Of the sight
That creates
Gratitude
For simplicity

The sound of waves
Has me singing a tune
The ocean dwelling
Electrifies my soul
With harmonious lyrics
Captivating melodies
It's a grand escape
Into liberation
When I watch
The sun go down
Without one to love
But I'm in love with the sea
My favorite place to be
I sing with the waves
And dance with the stars
As the sun went down
The moon came up
And I'm out here
Changing with the tide
Because my heart found home
When I threw out the anchor
To let my soul drift
With the currents
Of wave motion
The wave music
Moves within me
Into the night sky

His marvelous creation
Made for us to enjoy
Is taken for granted
Society destroys
The natural world
The purest of elements
Are overrun by toxins
The clean air
Polluted by chemicals
The mighty trees
Uprooted in masses
The remarkable ocean
Flooded with oil
The whole earth
Littered by careless fools
Who worship progression
Who become technology's slaves
They no longer
Cherish the gift
He provided
And even shared
Some of Himself with us
The wind is His caressing breath
The trees His strong-rooted love
The mountains His unshakable care
The ocean His powerful energy
Nature belongs to the Creator
And man ruins
His artwork

Instant connections
Like the flow
Of water moving
In the same direction
A natural surge
Of charged energy
Attracted to the ebb
Retreating from loneliness
To the comfort
Of another's arms
Moved together
But separated
Like a slipstream
You were a daydream
Can only stare
At the swells
For so long
Before departure
Before a drought

As I look to the sky
Searching for answers
Some aspect of clarity
For my purpose here
I am granted a peace
By the layer of blue
That wraps me up
In comforting arms
The fresh air
Pours into my lungs
Refreshing and revitalizing
The question of why
Escapes my mind
Like clouds rolling by
So that I instead
Dwell in acceptance
Of what is
The atmosphere, the earth
The fact I'm one in billions
And even if my name
Is never known
At least I'm famous
To the sky
Staring down at me

Crystal water gleams
While sunlight streams
The waves rolling
A magic calling
Awakening the soul
Vibrant and whole
In an ocean caress
Relieved of stress
A salt rejuvenation
Like a new creation
Enlightened with serenity
Detached from identity
Solely being
Wholly seeing
The majestic sea
A Mother devotee
In the true abode

The trees that bloom
Under the luminous moon
By the silver river
Where dreams shimmer
In pools of aspirations
Drifting leaves of revelations
Long sought after
Nature's answer
To the yearning
For more meaning
Sent to the empyrean
From the lips of a fantasian
A mystical venture
To find spiritual treasure
Discovering the truth
Like the devoted sleuth
To follow the bold moon
And reach soon
The silver river
That will deliver
The sought after dreams
Long forgotten it seems

The trees speak
In tender whispers
Reminders of awareness
To look up
From that device
Compelling its user
And instead
Dwell in nature
The real surroundings
See the leaves
How they gladly dance
By kiss of the breeze
How they brightly smile
By touch of sunlight
See the branches
How they stretch out
Strong and confident
With no expectations
And the stump of the tree
Taking the burden
Of supporting the beauty
The storms that come
Try to break the strength
And destroy the structure
Of that tough tree
But it perseveres
Knowing that soon
The sun will shine
And the branches
Won't feel so heavy
The leaves will sing
A joyous song again
Because as a whole
The tree is strong
And it loves
Every season of life
(cont.)

People could be the same
But those staring at a screen
Won't learn how
To bear fruits
If they don't
Look up

My soul is filled
With an inner-present calm
As I sit and meditate
In the peace of nature
My mind is relaxed
And I feel a connection
Wonderful and powerful
Is this link
That I reach alignment
Able to grasp intricacies
Touch, sight, thoughts
I sense the elements
Wind awakening me
Trees refreshing me
Ocean reviving me
Sun soothing me
And my presence marvels
At the adjoining of earth
With one soul
Who simply closed thy eyes
And called on the mystic
Spirit of nature
Which I found thee
Within me

LOVE CHARMS

I love the taste
Of your name
On my lips
I say it repeatedly
My body igniting
With the ringing sparks
Of letters and sound
Adjoining together
Forming the word
That is your name
Oh to speak it
Sends tingles down my spine
As if I can imagine
Your fingertips
Trailing down every vertebrae
Oh to say it
Sends warmth through my bones
As if I can feel
Your tender skin
Enveloping every inch of mine
Your name
Is magic

Water my heart
Like a garden
I am a delicate flower
In need of a drink
Your eyes are the sun
The light I need
Your arms are the soil
The blanket I desire
Your lips are the bees
The touch I yearn
So water my heart
Stare lovingly at me
Wrap me in your skin
Taste honey on my lips
Don't love me simply
Be the garden
In which I grow
Be my roots
Love me strong

Somehow you are
The only reason
I'm still alive
Your heart beats for me
Your lungs breathe for me
Waking up
To see your eyes
Is what keeps me
From drowning
Into the abyss
Of my misery
Your sweet soul
Is the only link
For mine to stay
And I wash
Away my pain
By getting drunk on you
Tasting the joy on your lips
Feeding off your happiness
Wrapping myself up
In your warmth
Hoping to steal
Some of your light
To ease the darkness
That haunts my mind

You are gold to me
Not the kind worn
But the hour
When the sun ignites
With yellow brilliance
Showering the earth
In glorious beauty
Dazzling light
Like true magic
Sparkling pixie dust
Raining down warmth
Radiating kindness
Like your smile
And tender eyes
Full of hope
For when the sun sets
And your wild comes out

A firelight serenade
Words of devotion
Dancing like the flames
A multicolored world
Hued with yellow, orange
And red, love spreading
This wildfire burns
Brighter, quicker
Coruscating shadows
Bodies intertwined
Surrounded by smoke
Breathe deeply in
And lost within
Skin, music, light
Hallucinations
Of stars around
Adding to the groove
The embers never dim
Not when arms entangle
And mouths adjoin
The fire never ends
When I'm with you

From a simple touch
There was a connection
As if currents of electricity
Were powered by fingertips
And the warmth of skin
The channel by which it flowed
My battery was almost empty
But you filled it to full
Like a sudden switch flipped
And the light turned on
You awoke within me
A certain recharge of purpose
And though my forte
Will never be electrical
I feel a flow of energy
Imagined to be quite similar
To the bond we formed
But as you walked away
Someone dimmed the lights
And pulled the plug
For once I felt sorrow
Over loss of power
Though I don't need it
I certainly need you
For us together
Would be bold and real
As lightning across the sky
We light up the atmosphere
Brighter than a storm
Than the fourth of July
Than the flames of sun
We are the surge
So phenomenally astounding
That the universe ignites
And explodes with waves
Of incomprehensible love

I am the lone wolf
Howling at the moonlight
You hunt me with words of adoration
And to you I willingly run
Into the forest of your eyes
One I want to get lost in
Tangled in branches
Surrounded by trees
Like your arms wrapped around me
And your skin enveloping me
The animals inside of us
Nourished by each other
Dance with me by the moon
We are the wolves
Creatures of the night
Together by the call
The work of the wild

You are the ocean
I am the waves
Together we are whole
Without my swells
You are flat
Without your water
I am empty
You need my energy
Like I need your salt
You need my love
Like I need your heart

Try to resist you
But I fail miserably
Withholding emotions
Chaining up feelings
Screaming for liberty
In the midst of drought
I suffer unquenchable thirst
A dire need for you
To feel your body
Woven into mine
For eventually rain
Must fall
In the desert
Like I
Must pour
Into your arms

Run fingers through my hair
I can't seem to get air
My body is tingling
Struck with certain feeling
Your smiles make me warm
I'm flattered by your charm
Like someone I've known forever
You give me butterflies like never
So much uncertain
But fate might be ascertain
That we belong together
Our hearts strung like a tether

Dewdrops on roses
Like wine-stained lips
Get drunk on my soul
And we'll crash like waves
Wind blowing trees
Like whispers of affection
Your face on my neck
And your hands on my spine
Birds sweetly singing
Like the sound of heartbeats
A solar eclipse
Like a new set passion
Your eyes are my sea
And I dive right in
Oh let me fall like rain
Into your embrace
Sand prickling skin
Like the touch of fingertips
A scorching dessert
Like temperature rising
Get lost in my soul
And we'll fly like Aves
Into a sky of shooting stars
Like the motion of our bodies
When you're dazed by the feeling
You can have the whole world

She is a delicate flower
Touch her tenderly
So her petals don't fall
Hold her softly
So she doesn't wilt
Speak to her sweetly
So you won't see her thorns
So her beauty never ceases
Love her with passion
So she is never thirsty
Be always by her side
So her roots are firm
Be her sunshine
That brightens her color
That helps her grow
Kiss her with your light
So that she radiates with joy
Be the soil that shapes her
That nourishes her soul
So that she stands proud
So that she feels secure
In your arms
Love your delicate flower
For she is the seed
Of everlasting possibility

When I think of you
It scares me
Because suddenly
I'm overwhelmed
With confusing emotions
The time we first met
By the fire at night
I thought maybe
You could be mine
But just as the seasons change
We both changed
As if we allowed
The unfriendly weather
To tear us apart
You moved on
Like the happening
Of winter trees
Ok with losing their leaves
Barren with loneliness
I could have tried
To catch your leaves
To grasp onto hope
Like the promise of spring
And express my feelings
Like flowers blooming
Growing the heart with love
But I was uncertain
You were unsure
Like a storm
Battling the sun
Over who gets the sky
Maybe both of us
Could have won
If we decided
To share the thoughts
That could have overpowered
The chaotic weather
With a rainbow

The ocean he tastes
So fresh on my lips
Speckled with salt
I speak to him
In the song of Neptune
Proclaiming loud
I the daughter of the sea
A fish out of water
Kiss the land dweller
Just to pull him under
My eyes lure him
My words like a trident
To which I control
The waves of love
From drowning us both

Even though you're far
I think of you
Constantly imagining
The looks of your face
Inches from mine
How your blonde locks
Dust your forehead
Your tender blue eyes
Are the ocean I yearn
The soft feel of your lips
Are the drink
That quenches my thirst
Every part of you
Every intricate detail
I adore, I remember
And when I picture you
Right beside me
I can feel the warmth
Of your hand
Tattooed with an anchor
Of my heart
Being the force
That keeps me from drifting
Too far
You are too far
But you are a part of me
And I in you
So shall we sail
Our ship of love
Into eternal seas
Of glorious ecstasy

I wonder if you'll love me
Like the birds
The inseparable bond
Between gentle creatures
The chirp of pleasure
At sight of their lover
The instinctual care
And desire of togetherness
For thou and I united
Sing me a song
Words of tender adoration
And we'll soar
Into starry skies
As I look into your eyes

I'd love to dive
Into your depths
To see the world
From a grander view
Belonging to you
Fully knowing you
Understanding you
Memorizing every feature
As if I were the diver
Studying the ocean
Marveling at your soul
The mystical traits
That form your personality
And the deeper I go
The less I want to leave
So would you take me
Into your arms
Would you succumb me
In an oceanic embrace

They warned me
Not to tattoo
Your name
On my body
Because the letters
Would be permanent
But that's how
I wanted you
On my skin
On my mind
In my life
Forever
Until death
Do us part
Come back
Stay
Like the ink
Permanent
On my skin
In my heart
Forever

All these presents
Stacked under the tree
So much anticipation
For materialistic pleasures
But all I want
Is a little bit of nature
And a lot of you
Hang the mistletoe
Come into my arms
Let me unwrap
The greatest gift of all
Every inch of you

My innocent side
Accepted the view of clothes
And embraced the covered you
But my rebellious side
Taunted by lustful pleasure
Stripped you bare
Down to naked skin
I pictured you raw
And admired for a while
Until I yearned for more
And went deeper
Pulled back the skin
To observe your heart
The intricate character
Traits, emotions, history
That shaped you
All for my knowledge
So that every part of you
Belongs to me
And now so shall I
Undress for you

Every second
We grow older
Which means
Without you
Time is wasted
Every minute
Death draws nearer
Every hour
Turns into
Every day
And suddenly
Months go by
Years
Need more of you
I can't die
Without you
In my arms
For more than
A moment

I'd love to explore
The vast expanse
Of your wild mind
To understand the thoughts
Every vivid image
Created solely by you
And every single feeling
Your beautiful body exhibits
I'd love to memorize
Those fantastical emotions
As a fluent song
To know you more
Than even you know yourself
I'd love to swim
In a pool of your memories
To partake in your nostalgia
For you are my reason
My purpose for living
And even if your brain
Was washed in madness
I'd still adore you
Because that would add
Another thing
We have in common
We fell in love
Truth be told
Guess I already know your mind
And I'm drunk on you

As you trace
The contour of my face
And I feel the warmth
Of tender fingertips
I can't help but revel
At the sensation
Of your alluring touch
Provoking within me
A sinful desire
The urge to have
More of your skin
To discover you
At greater depths
And as our heartbeats
Pound in the rhythm of love
I can see the embers
In your compelling eyes
Waiting to be fed
To ignite with the flames
That I'll cause to burn
All you have to do
Is take a drink
Of my lips
And don't stop indulging
Until thirst is quenched

Fused to the euphoric visionary
Gazing at the sky in meditation
As if he sat above the clouds
Soaring beyond the limitations
With profound intellectual level
A shaman to the obsolete world
Words of robust ritual seep his lips
And skin is decorated with expressive art
Here the epitome of individuality lies
And I marvel at our connected sense
His jubilant love and care for one's soul
Shares the space of a pirate's heart
A whimsical voyager on the ship of awareness
I stay beside him on the enlightened path
We distinguish the truth from society
To follow the transcendental calling
Aligning our true journey with the stars
The energy of credibility flows between us
And so prudent minds adjoined as lovers
To cultivate within our synchronized beliefs
We plunge into the eyes of each other's
In the expanse of mystic ruminations
The life of deliverance within ourselves
Found by linking to the inner psyche
My ethereal mate is my complement
And now his fingers entangle mine

To soulful jazz
Spin me around
Softly whisper
Words of love
From wine-stained lips
And eyes of affection
Beam with pleasure
As we dance
To instrument melody
Our bodies in rhythm
A harmonious night
Of swaying, grinning
Falling for you
Over again
To soulful jazz
You carried me

As the sun sets
I see a future moment
Walking along the shore
Watching the waves crash
The sound of surging energy
Rushing through our bones
He holds my hand
With soft devotion
Like the salt water
Smooth on my skin
The one beside me
Is a prince of Poseidon
The ocean is a part of him
As it is a part of me
I wanted one who holds a trident
Now he holds my heart too
I wanted one who gazes at the horizon
Now he gazes at me too
I wanted one who rests on the beach
Now he rests beside me too
We listen to wave music
And fall in love over again
Us and the ocean

You decided on goodbye
Now I'll be
The crinkled picture
In your pocket
Just a memory
Of a long lost lover
With a broken soul
Once put back together
By tender hands
But then forgotten
And torn again
Soon you'll find
Just a photo
Crumbled in your pocket
A reminder
Of what you left
And what you miss

Your lips inches away
A playful smirk of desire
Adhering to the urge
To close the space between us
And my heart pounds
Tingles shoot down my spine
At the touch of your fingertips
And your arms envelop me
Suddenly we are one seed
Planting our roots in sheets
Sprouting with vigorous love
Growing as a tree our souls thrive
Until we reach the sky of stars
That light the path of ecstasy
To wish upon a comet of lust
As we're succumbed by galactic gleams
Taken far into a vast galaxy
Where time does not reach us
And we're together forever
We are a creation of nature
Budding a new dawn of existence

My soul is old
Found on long ago principles
Like the oasis of simplicities
Genuine acts such as thee
Picking a lovely flower
More meaningful than store bought gifts
And your time with me
Precious over any jewelry piece
I'd prefer your eyes
Over a screen's blue light
For your face is much more appealing
And your voice a lot more intriguing
So let us dance together
Under a dim candlelit room
Or under view of the moon
To antique records
That truly speak of passion
Eventually to fall asleep
In comfort of each other's arms
Astounded I am by your chivalry
And real essence of innocence
That the brilliantly unique you
Is my eternal companion
We are old souls
Together

Long and deep talks
To discover more of you
The way our minds relate
The way our thoughts
Harmonize
Like our voices
When you strum
And our notes collide
Complementing each other
Like our personalities
Our same intellect
Our music
I admire
The workings of your brain
The words you speak
Every letter, sound
The way you sing
Every simple moment
I fall more in love
With my favorite song
That is you

Lovely red lips
I painted for you
A tight black dress
I picked for you
Hoping you'd croon
At the sight of me
Take my hand
And fly me away
To the moon
A place to stay
In your embrace
To be kissed
More times than
The number of stars
Surrounding us
Twinkling lovers joy
A reflection
Of feeling
Alone together
In our own
Universe

Two souls linked
From across the globe
Found each other
Quite unexpectedly
A random meeting
That sent off sparks
An instant attraction
Deeper than first sight
An intimate connection
As if known forever
Like the same person
Who found the half
That made them whole
Such a blaze emanated
From the collision of hearts
That wisdom exploded
Ridding their sense of mind
To dwell in another world
Where all that exists
Is the inner psyches
Of eternal adoration

"She is of the sky
A celestial being
I tremble
At the sight of"
He wrote
Staring at
The polaroid photo
On his desk
A nostalgia
In monochrome
Her eyes and smile
Ignited the photo
As if it were in color
"Her radiant presence
Like empyreal sunrise
Angelic in her ways
As if a halo
Were her jewelry
I fell for
A winged beauty
A charismatic gem
But she was called
Back home
Where she belongs
In Heaven
Now where my heart is"
He looked at the paper
And the photo
With streaming tears
Not leaving the desk
Until he closed his eyes
And met her again

You are lovely
Though many don't realize
Because that precious voice
Barely speaks a word
To those it doesn't know
Shy and mysterious you are
Your words pour out to me
Like a rushing river
Excited and full of energy
Yet you hide all the layers
All the depth I adore
How did I get so lucky
That you reveal
The side to me
No one else gets
The pleasure to have

Alive in you
Burying my face
In your chest
Feeling the warmth
Of your skin
Smooth and moist
Dripping in beads
Of lustrous energy
Lips meshed
In a boisterous song
Hearts as one
Rhythmic drumbeat
A rowdy tempo
Of electric coitus
Belonging to you
Thrilling ecstasy
Last forever
As one
With my love

It was an accident
To love your bare skin
As much as I did
The first time
For the times I resisted
The times you persisted
And the day we married
I realized the years
Of holding back
Lead to the moment
Of letting go
So suddenly I dove
Farther than ever
Scaring you with passion
And thrilling your desire

Like playing a piano
I want to stroke the keys
Of your heart
To hear the sweet sound
Of my favorite notes
That are your features
Each breath, every smile
Motions of expression
The finest tune of song
Your voice plays
Ringing in my ears
Generating adoration
For my treasured instrument
Love bursts forth in music
A striking anthem of ecstasy
In your rhythmic embrace

Places a flower
In her hair
Touches her cheek
Kisses her there
Lovely lady
He adores
Precious body
He adorns
Not with jewels
Nor diamonds
But with flowers
Because nature
Is not only
More beautiful
Than things
It is priceless
Just like her

Try to suppress
The animal instincts
But when I see you
I want to drink up
Every inch of skin
And claim it as mine
Having no control
Over the aching pains
That yearn for you
For bodies to be one
For hearts to collide
And minds to unite
And feelings to ignite
Staring at you
Is the most brutal
Suffering in want
Watching from a distance
Dreaming of being yours
Wrapped in arms
Tied in tongues
My imagination
Seems so real
And yet all I know
Is the taste of your name
On my lips
But I want you
My gosh I want you

Your face is intoxicating
Your body is exhilarating
You arouse me
And my feelings give
Like the sky falling
To crush me under
The weight of love
In the pressure
Of your embrace
In the presence
Of your energy
The sparks could kill
But instead they thrill
All the sense I had
Gone into your skin
It feels like a sin
An evocative bliss
I can't miss
Forever it must be
You and me
For eternity

While she sits and stares
She wanders
In her mind
Forming visions
Of a fairytale
A perfect romance
But simply
She just wants
Someone to love
To love her
To hold her
To tell her
How much
She is worth
To adventure with her
Experience life with her
And be her best friend
She wonders
Why it's so hard
To find someone
She questions herself
How she looks
How she acts
And hopes that
It will be enough
For someone
To accept her
To be the one
She sees
In her mind
And wishes
To call hers

Felt the throb
In my core
The urgency
In my bones
To touch you
To hold you
To be one
We connected
Like magnets
Glances of desire
Smiles of yearning
If only
We were brave
And admitted
The truth
There was a spark
Deeper than physical
Stronger than mental
The truth
I crave you
I can't live
Without you

I studied you
From a distance
And fell in love
With your looks
Knowing nothing
But the feel
Of your name
On my lips
And the view was exciting
Until the ship sailed by
You drifted away
As the speck in the horizon
I mourned the departure
As the last image
Disappeared from sight
Now I regret not knowing
Not climbing aboard the ship
To discover you
So I'm left with a dream
A hopeless desire
To see you again
If I see you again
I'd chase after you
Not lose sight of the ship
Grasp more than just a name

You're a bad influence
On my mental health
My physical condition
But I'm in love with
The rebel in you
Adorable drunk
Laughing hysterically
Playing me naughty
And smoke rings
Sifting out your lips
Tickling my face
The smell of herbs
The sense of earth
All around me
In your arms
Decorated with art
Your rough edges
I found soft
All your gritty pleasures
I found thrilling
You are intoxicating
And I can't seem
To get enough
Of the buzz
I feel when I'm with you
Like a poison
I shouldn't drink
I chug
And have
Reverse effect
Coming alive
From what should scare
From what should kill
I take the risk
I run to you
Over and over
Again

The river flows smooth
Against the rocks
Like the sound of your voice
Meeting my ears
Or the feel of your skin
Softly brushing mine
As the clear water moves
With a tender current
Your lovely presence
Drifts closer in a delicate air
You are the elemental phenomenon
Of liquid energy
Surging with purpose
To accomplish the goals
To find the love
Headed in a straight direction
Clear and clean from distraction
Carrying on the mission
You flow like the river
Let me be the rocks
You pour your magic over

I love when
Your eyebrow raises
And the side
Of your mouth
Curves into a smirk
The leading signs
Of mischievous behavior
That thrills me
With curiosity
So that I wish
To open the door
Of your mind
Step inside
And see your thoughts
Memorize every detail
Because the more
I discover you
The less I'll want
To turn back
The more I desire
To close the door
And never come
Back out

She's a mystery
You're hoping to solve
But like a puzzle
With missing pieces
There are parts of her
You're missing too
So in order
To put her together
You must find
The hidden bits
The lost gems
The broken pieces
Accept the imperfections
The rough edges
Be willing
To fix them
With healing hands
That care enough
To see
The finished puzzle
The solved mystery
Completed

Fingertips of moonlight
Trail across my skin
As if the kiss of stars
Weren't enough to hold me
The passion went infinite and beyond
Wrapped in your arms of heaven
It feels like a galactic reverie
Getting lost in your planet
While the sky still dazzles
With your breaths on my neck
And the ship to get to
This intimate space
Seemed so frightening
Until we broke the surface
The view, the feel
Was so marvelous
That when we landed
Even the pull of gravity
Couldn't keep us apart

The sight of you
Reminded me of our
Long summer nights
When we became
Wild animals
Roaming the sandy shores
Of our favorite beach
Watching the sunset
Drinking cherry rum
And seeing our smoke
Dance to the pink sky
Until it became dark
And you held me
In a perfect embrace
While we gazed at stars
And after the heat
Perspired from our bodies
In that close space
We threw off our clothes
And ran fearlessly
Naked and free
Into the ocean
Where we got lost
In waves, salt, and skin

You are the picturesque image
I see in my dreams
A sort of icon
Representing all my hopes
For what I seek
In my ethereal mate
Someday soon
As the visionary
With a sacred effigy
Pieced in my mind
I hope to find you
To see you face to face
To uncover the truths
Of this foresight
So what's in my mind
Becomes a reality

I just want to
Want to feel
Feel your arms
Wrapped around me
Your soft skin
Against mine
And my head
On your chest
Listening to the sound
Of your heartbeat
While your fingers
Run through my hair
Belonging to you
Soaking up your
Your intoxicating embrace
Like a comforting blanket
I never want to leave
The warmth that fixed
Fixed my cold soul
You knocked down
Down the walls
I always put up
Never let anyone in
Until you came
And persisted
To see the other side
The side I tried to hide
You get to hold
Forever in
In your arms

Your mind I adore
The depth it goes
The profundity of your thoughts
Words of sagacity on your lips
The way you think
Aligns with the insight
I meditate on
Ponder
Reflect
Ruminate
And I never believed
Someone like you
Would find me
And understand me
Because I needed
One who wasn't scared
To leave the shallows
But these days
It's almost impossible
To find people
Who are willing
To swim
Without being able
To touch
The bottom
While I lose sight
Of the ground
You do too
And it's a thrill
To go deep
With you

Your fingertips feel
Like the soft leaves
Of autumn falling
The burst of color
That ignites the sky
My delicate skin
With dazzling brilliance
The scenery
And kind of delight
I want to nurture
To keep alive
Before they fade
Before they leave
My spine
And I'm left
With emptiness
So much space
Between us
Between the branches
Until you come back
With green revival
To fill the sky
And touch me
All over again
As the seasons change

I await the bliss
Of reuniting with you
Letting the sand
Run through my fingers
Of your golden hair
Letting the ocean
Rush through my veins
When I dive into
Your azure eyes
May you be mine
In the deep seas
Because I'm not
The kind of person
To remain in the shallows
I'd much rather
Be wrapped in
The depths of your arms
And let the salt
From your lips
Be my only breath

As sunshine beams
Kiss your skin
Smooth and rich
Sweet like honey
Melt into my arms
Pour your passion
Of fresh springs
Herbal wilderness
Fields of flowers
Earthy exhilaration
Into me
So that my senses
Ignite with nature
Revived by your touch
Growing stronger by
Your intimate roots
Coming alive
By untamed behavior
The natural forms
Raw and untouched
Are more invigorating
Than subdued
Which is why
I love you wild

BOLD EXPLORERS

Gazing out the home window
Wondering if a grand thing
Might happen this routine day
For if opportunity came
As a thrill knocking at the door
I'd gladly open my mind
To accept the path of adventure
This wanderlust heart is hungry
And won't be satisfied until
The brink of riveting exploration
Knowingly came to rescue me
Instead of living through pages
I enter a life of experiences
But here I still am
Staring out the home window
Dreaming of far-off places
Getting lost in unknown lands
Pretending the blue sky an ocean
And the harsh cold ceased to exist
Darkness comes with the sunset
But I'm waiting for a grand thing
Maybe tomorrow it shall come
On another routine day

There she was
Lost in dreams
Cascading around her
Like roaring seas
A breath of air
A whisper of winds
Liberates her soul
To soar high
With the wings
You can't see
Watch out
She is free

Shall I pack tonight
It won't take long
Never did I need much
Nor want a lot
But I've been waiting
For the chance
To leave for long
I'd waste it all
The degree, the job
The house, the car
All gone
For an adventure
To find deliverance
From the greed
From the impurity
From the bounds of society
I'd go with you
I'd live daringly
Just ask me
Take the risk
Jump over the edge
And I'd follow
Because not only
Do I seek the thrill
And the freedom of outdoors
I yearn to discover
What it feels like
To go wild with you

Constant daydreams
Of a faraway place
Where you aren't
But where you want to be
Feelings of deep yearning
A desire to break free
Trapped at home
But not a true haven
That place so out of reach
You want to grasp
Onto those dreams
But unsure how
To make visions actual
And while your soul cries
And your heart grows weary
Imagine you are there
Where you ought to be
Pretend to smell the flowers
Or walk through open fields
Dip your toes in the ocean
Or relax in the sand
Climb a tall mountain
Or gaze from great heights
Escape in thick forests
Or listen to sounds of the woods
Trudge through icy snow
Or watch the flakes gently fall
Get lost in the desert
Or tour ancient sites
Drive in the busy city
Or stroll amidst the bright lights
Wherever you want to be
Is where you ought to go
To live in the land unhappy
Is to die a worthless life
For no man can feel alive
(cont.)

If they dwell in a trap
No soul can thrive
If it belongs somewhere else
Listen to the daydreams
The voices in your head
The whispers from your heart
And go where you desire
So that special haven
Is no longer a dream

Feel the energy of winds
Shifting through like a tide
The wave currents of life
Fluctuating the days in mystery
That distant horizon of wonder
Promising a new dawn of existence
Sprouts within a voyager heart
A brink of desire from the salt
From the depths of the soul
A sailor shall rise to seek a journey
And cast away the anchor once residing
So to embark on a true calling
The heart that dwells on a pirate's ship
Has some hallucination of a quest
On the search for more than gold
To travel, to see, to explore
The restless spirit of a born mariner
Lets the winds lead his natural essence
And departs the unfitting shore
Here now the adventure lies
Grab the rum
And get on board

The storms of life
Happen not to destruct
But to strengthen
Like climbing a mountain
Painful, but impactful
The heights ahead
Seem to be the enemy
But in actuality
The climbs motivate
Greater perseverance
To push through
Rough times
Arduous trials
Onerous struggles
Elements that steepen
Try to defeat
The hopeful climber
But push through
To reach the top
To look back
And see how far
Hope carried you
To reaching victory
See, the skies clear

Drift away in dreams
Where the nomad gleams
And escapes into the realm
Of no overwhelm
To find serenity
To stay for eternity
Where the world is absent
But nature is present
A place to roam the earth
In euphoric rebirth
To connect with the spirit
And have no limit
A soul finally free
To just damn be

Torn between identities
As if wanting to be everything
But thinking only one thing
Is all that's allowed
When a wide range
A collage of variety
A multicolored canvas
Is much more interesting
Than one bland quality
Following multiple paths
Is a lot more adventurous
Than one certain path
Be it all
The artist, the athlete, the genius
Wherever the calling leads
Follow the passion
Do the things
That ignite within
A burning pleasure
Delightful flames of light
Shine through to show
A joyful life of satisfaction
Lived to the fullest
Reached by courageous acts
Of being fearless
Of being everything
All in one

Mystic waves of exploration
Flow within me new direction
The movement of the tide
Awake my soul to never hide
I seek the faraway horizon
As the sun will surely brighten
Traverse athwart the ocean
Swayed by currents of motion
So shall I discover totality
By sailing away from normality
Oh speak to me wondrous surf
Align the journey to which I morph
The path to indigenous freedoms
Found in the native kingdoms
An esoteric escapade
To some distinct everglade
Absent the world of plastic people
Now removed from the upheaval
To roam throughout natural earth
Feels like marvelous rebirth
My voyage among the waves
Has saved me from the graves

Angelic music
Move within me
Shake these bones
With majestic vibrations
The sound of gold
Fill my ears
With sweet ringing
Reach my soul
To feel the thrill
Of pure harmony
All the joyous melodies
Like a symphony
For my core elements
Fundamental pieces
To connect with buoyant notes
Oh seraphic music
Flow within me
Kindle the passion
To burst forth
Out from my body
The current spreads
To ethereal dance
To dulcet singing
High on lyrical tunes
I become the song

Midnight dreamer
Ventures in fantasy
A roaming soul
A mind lost in stars
Altered by illusions
Euphoria in the magic
The splendid escape
In a world of color
A chromatic canvas
Painted reveries
Close thy eyes
And drift away

Let me go back
To child-like wonder
Let me stare out
The window
Awaiting the arrival
Of Peter Pan
He'll take me
Far away
To Neverland
Even more appealing
Now older and grown
I wish to return
To youthful bliss
The adventurous spirit
Of wild imagination
Free to roam
Without forced ties
To job, money, stress
The ways of the world
Give every reason
To leave elsewhere
And be a kid again
I'd happily fight the pirates
Dance with the fairies
Face the ticking crocodile
Live wildly under the stars
If it meant
I could stay young
Forever I would, and I could
Grasp the hand of Pan
Soar among the clouds
Bask in the sunlight
Fly across the sky
With a trail of pixie dust
And an eternal smile
On my innocent face
(cont.)

As I become
One of the Lost Boys
Here now Peter Pan
I stare out my window
Come take me
To Neverland
My heart cries out
For you
To save me
From the prison
Of reality

The traveler seeks unfamiliar paths
Broadening his horizons on an escapade
Discovering the glorious liberty
Of fleeing social chains
Ridding himself of the clerical enterprises
Discarding his erstwhile greed of money
Relinquishing his luxurious automobile
Cleansing himself of technological progression
Stripping his posh garments of class
Disowning his fancy of swank life
Repulsed, he deserts the plastic-people character
And follows the indubitable journey of deliverance
He delves into the wild for restoration
For nature shall repair what society broke
He will cease to be a conformist
For the raw earth will enlighten him
Like a phoenix rising from the ashes
He is reborn with newfound savagery
His spirit fearlessly roams in nakedness
Emotions and expressions now unclothed
His destiny completely belongs to him
The actions, decisions, and thoughts unfiltered
He thrives in the prelapsarian wilderness
Every minuscule thought of previous living now obliterated
His wandering feral spirit found its dawning in nature
And he will be the faithful explorer till the end of time

Dreaming instead of doing
Seemingly the only escape
From life's strongholds
The true route of deliverance
Found in the mind's own compass
Without individual direction
There presents nothing but lies
Vying for irrelevant attention
To the fraught routine
Of the naïve common man
Wasting away their hours
Like a flock of sheep
Grazing every day
Trapped in a prison fence
Locked into doing
Like a machine built
Within society's gates
But the dreamers
Refuse to be trapped
To be stuck in a pasture
So they roam in endless fields
With far expanding horizons
Because they won't allow
Anyone to build a fence
Around their mind

Life with you is adventurous
Because every action
I take beside you
Leads me closer to fearless
Your daring heart tore down
Every wall that I allowed
To trap me within the dark
You brought me into the light
And now I'm vibrantly alive
The urge for venturing
Is at its heights
I'm willingly ready to climb
Whether it be steep or not
I'll take on the challenge
Though I've already won
You and I are exploring
The world together
Forever let's trek
As nomadic soul mates
We are free to go
Wherever, whenever
Wanderers
Fearlessly
On the move

Poetic words of vision
Escape the stargazer's lips
Scattering like constellations
So the artful mind expands
Like the drape of night sky
Reflected in her eyes
And planetary illusions
Hidden within her gaze
She talks of outer space
As if the excursion
Is already planned
The writings and daydreams
Seen from telescopic view
Though she knows one day
A rocket will take her
Far away, away far
If you want to keep her
Don't leave her
To look at stars alone
Because she loves the sky
And might choose
Her galactic reveries
And pursuit of infinity
Over the enclosure
Of your arms

The risk is thrilling
Letting everything go
In hopes of winning it all
Achieving victory of goals
Making dreams a reality
Hopes and desires reached
But without the daring endeavor
Of sacrificing normal traditions
One will never find fulfillment
In the stereotypical comfort zone
So step out of the box
Break out of the chains
Society placed on each individual
For on the edge of spontaneous drive
Those who take the leap
Are sure to land
Where no one else has
And that is where
Success meets the champion

Reality is normality
So on the brink of decision
Between the path of others
Or my own created route
The unknown trail
Is a thrilling risk
That I yearn to take
To jump over the edge
Instead of hesitating the fall
For the rush is exhilarating
Uncertainty is captivating
And whenever I land
In some crazy dream of mine
I'm pleased that I chose
My reality as abnormality

A grand getaway
I hope for someday
Soon to have a break
From the chaos I make
Life becomes crazy
And times of being lazy
Are small, but judged
As if I never budged
But exhaustion lurks
While there are smirks
Acting as if tiredness
Were a crime of weariness
Yet everyone relates
We all carry weights
Searching for relief
To replace the grief
A reason why
I'd say bye
And sail away
From the stressors bay

A path unmarked by footprints
The uncarved tree
The unseen creek
Form the unknown land
An untraveled route
Is the one I seek
No eyes have discovered
The mystery yielded
Coaxed by the prodigious earth
To embark on a solitary thrill
No settler rests within me
Colonization generates civilization
Yet the wanderer thrives in liberation
A maverick I am to roaming
Because the nomad learns at optimum
More of the world's knowledge
Than the institution lectures
And swank living they adore
Not for the gypsy heart
Restless and yearning for deliverance
The call of the wild comes in a song
A freeing tune to always sing
On the path now marked
By one set of footprints

A pirate's lullaby
I sing to the breeze
Salty hair blowing
Cracked lips open
Liquor on my breath
Hat upon my head
Blue eyes fixated
On the wide horizon
Ship amongst the waves
Sails into the skies
And the Captain
With a sailor's mouth
Yells cheerful jeers
How he loves
To be at sea
Red-skinned
Carefree
Ocean scoundrel
Ridding of land
And its crazy folk
To sail away
Never look back
Never return again
The pirate's life
Is the one for me

Told to find myself
A path to follow
Passion to pursue
Dream to chase
Told to express myself
Make decisions
Explore variety
Conquer fears
But the moment
I seem to find
An answer
A calling
It's as if
I were a wild animal
Taken from my freedom
Locked in a cage
Captive to the control
Of the one
Who won't let me go

Twinkling stars
Little specks of hope
Amidst the darkness
Promising the attainment
Of sought after dreams
That if reached for
Without shrouded focus
One will meet
And see the light
From a new perspective
Glorious achievement
To hold the aspiration
To embrace the gift
Time was spent
Searching and striving
Now to receive
The star of dreams
Real and vivid
In one's hands

"Stop living in your head
Little child"
They always say
But my imagination
Is the only escape
The only route of liberation
From the chaos
I travel the distant lands
Roam the far-off shores
In the stories I create
To ease the boredom
To release the shackles
Of materialistic things
That never mattered
I sail the desolate seas
Venture the wild jungles
Climb the tallest mountains
Trek the relentless deserts
See the outlandish places
All in daydreams
Wishing for that reality
Of a wanderer
A nomad
A pirate
A thrill-seeker
With a free spirit
And a reckless heart
Never afraid to take risks
Always on an adventure
Might the visions come true
If I never stop believing
Never stop dreaming
Soon to be living
What I see
In my head
Little child
Don't lose
Hope

Just a wrecked soul
Searching for answers
Wanting to understand
The purpose of life
Constant musing
Of what could be
Placing dreams and visions
On a scale of reality
Though the fantasy
Is more pleasant
The crave for insight
For depth and experience
Is a hunger
Strong enough
That giving up
Wasn't an option
Discovering the truth
Was more important
Than giving in
To the same routine
As those who
Live in a box
Don't they see
That even with
The carried pain
And many scars
A soul with
Broken pieces
That keeps on fighting
That ignites with curiosity
And opens up
To the world
With arms outstretched
Lives a lot more
Adventurous and interesting
Traveling on a road
(cont.)

Without a certain destination
Than those who
Are too fearful
To take the risk
And go

Cigarettes burn
Close my eyes
And drift away
To the land
Of unexpected words
That connect and form
Bursting with emotion
Into the tales
The spellbinding stories
That explode with color
As if I were
Living them
Getting lost
In another world
Becomes a passion
Creative vibrancy
Seeps into the smoke
Like a rainbow
It's a rush
Somehow formed
In my mind
From the breaths
Words on my lips
On the paper
By the wine
With the jazz
It sets the tune
For the mood
In a poet's world
And here now
Lives the poem

Ready to go
To spread my wings
And fly away
Adventure calls
I wish to answer
Nature speaks
I wish to reply
Nomadic exploration
Wanderlust cravings
To see the world
Travel infinitely
Nurture the soul
That cries for thrills
For riveting experiences
For rousing discoveries
To let loose
To take risks
Bold and daring
Pushing the limits
Learning how to be
Fearless
I'm ready
Leaving soon
Not looking back

MYSTERIOUS HUMANS

Moments slip by
Yet we let them
The seconds fall
Quick like raindrops
Bursting on impact
From the ground's obliteration
Yet we let time go
Wasting it on unnecessaries
Forgetting to live
As if we might
Die tomorrow
We ought to get a jar
And hold it open
To catch the raindrops
To save the moments
Which make the memories
For a full jar
Presenting one
With a life
Of cherished
Seconds
Minutes
Hours
Days
Years
Until the end
Indeed comes

They shape you
To fit the mold
Those control freaks
They want to keep you
On puppet strings
Find the scissors
Cut them off
And dance away
All the worries
And the sickly stress
They gave you
Throw it all
In the trash
And never look back
At that garbage

Fragile figure
Corrupted by voices
Whispering lies
Famished bones
Never eating
Always seeing
Too much skin
Where it's lacking
Walking skeleton
Dead inside
Dying outside
Withering away
Refusing nourishment
Source of control
Until to dust
Now returning

There is a masterpiece
Happening within the eyes
Of every individual
One must look closer
To see beneath
The common surface
And gaze in awe
At the dazzling art
Of colorful emotions
On vivid display
For those who care
To grasp the depths
The history of life
Each canvas beholds
For within the pupils
Beyond the irises
Is a person's painting
Their past, present
Future aspirations
Painted by the growth
Blended by the story
Finished by the journey
Of the person
Who decided
To create their life
And live in color
The eyes
Are vibrant works
For those who care
To grasp the depths

If I were a drunkard
Would you still love me
Liquor always on my breath
The taste staining my lips
Intoxicating my mind
Waiting to corrupt me
Like an addictive drug
Streaming through my veins
My new way of euphoria
Suddenly no longer you
I never cared
Oh wait
I speak of you
And your violent eyes
Under influence
Who you used to be
Gone
And you think
I still love you
I want you
But you no longer exist
Your heart belongs
To the bottles
Your soul is captive
To a new lover
Alcohol
Stole you away from me

At dawn in the horizon
Renders an oasis of hope
Blazing rays of joyous light
Drown out the darkness
Brighten the life
Of a desolate soul
From the grim depths of despair
They shall rise like the sun
Painting the sky with color
With optimistic character
Becoming the exuberant rays
Spreading their beams out
To share the newfound gladness
Awakening the hearts still captive
That must break free
From the hell-like misery
Binding them to depression
Cast away the shackles
The tunnel comes to an end
Where light will be found
Sure as the night disappears
And the sun rises victoriously
So shall they
In hope, in time

The trees are said to be pleasant
But they're cut down
Like people who say they care
But judge the one who made a mistake
The ocean is found appreciated
But voluntarily polluted
Like people who say they love
But leave the one they promised
The grass is seen as beautiful
But it's destroyed
Like people who speak fanciful
But betray the one who trusted
Nature is said to be charming
But it's ruined
The hands of humankind
Destructive and back-stabbing
Selfish and greedy
If they really cared
If they really loved
Appreciated and kept their word
The earth would be left natural
They would be blissful
Magnificent rays of light
Would drown out their darkness

Vintage soul
They try to change you
With progressions
With inventions
But you hold onto the originals
Your heart belongs to the classics
The words form on your tongue
As you use the screen-less typewriter
The sound of a record player
Brings Presley to your ears
Antiques sit on your desk
Bell-bottoms are on your legs
You were born
In the wrong era
Vintage soul
They can't change you
Though they try to rearrange you
Saying time can't be reversed
Yet you found a way
To make the past stay
And you purse those red lips
With a daunting smirk
At those devices
That aren't your friends
Vintage soul
A collector's item
Worth more than gold

Never liked
Addictions
Controlling me
Owning every
Aspect
Captivating every
Thought
Would not
Allow
Handcuffs
Until I
Gave in
Temptation
Corrupted me
An unexpected
Storm
Relentless winds
Debauched me
Torrential rain
Flooded my
Sense

Human nature
So quick to believe
To fall captive
To the voices
In their head
That try to destroy
The confidence
Self-esteem
All the components
To have success
Deterred by the thoughts
Thinking "I'm not good enough"
"I can't do it"
When the reality is
Listening to the lies
Created by one's own mind
Must be stopped
How to gain control
Of the voices, thoughts
That destruct
Our inner being
From outward victory
Identify your worth
Calling and purpose
The little aspects
Of your identity
Connect to yourself
Find your voice
Let your wings spread
And fearlessly fly
With bold determination
To reach your goals
For a bright future
Think positive
Stop the voices
That hold you back
(cont.)

From potential
You can win the battle
You are worthy
Original
Amazing
Believe those truths

Darling
Let your tears fall
Like clouds releasing their bawl
At some time
The rain must pour
Like emotions
Need to soar

Dive into the depths
Be swallowed whole
By vast waters
Where voices are unheard
Except the ones
Consuming the mind
There is no escaping
The mental insanity
But breathe
And break free
You can escape
Their voices
The ones that try to change you
The ones that don't accept you
The ones that say you're unworthy
Dive into the depths
Where the only sound
Is rushing waters
Hopeful energy
No words
Only peace

Trees grow differently
Unique shapes and sizes
Certain angles
Special proportions
Some tall and thin
Others short and wide
Some with leaves and branches
Others nude and bare
But all trees
The same kind
Are authentically beautiful
So how come humans
Corresponding on earth
Shame physical distinctions
When they all
Grow like trees

They battle over paper
The monetary value
Stuffed in their pockets
Never meeting peace
Always trapped in greed
Spending and consuming
But never content
Staring at screens
To waste away their days
Losing their words
To the typing of thumbs
They gave their lives away
To follow the trends
All for the sake of image
And now they are becoming
The monsters that used to scare them
Their selfish acts
Are the world's destruction
And the only redemption
From the beast's snare
Is to let go
Of the things
That corrupted them
Love shall heal
The treacherous man
But he must find
In his heart
The desire
To care
For others
Again

The smell of coffee
Invigorates the senses
Fresh mornings of joy
With a cup in hand
Awaken the mind
For new possibilities
A whimsical world
Entered with caffeine
Pulsing through the veins
What a delight
Found in a second round
Grind the beans
That ground the day
The taste of pleasure
That creates fireworks
For the entire being
To come alive
From a simple drink
The greatest medicine
The cure to slumber
A true best friend

Your life is a canvas
Create yourself
Design your path
Paint your future
And leave space
For the unexpected
Don't let the world
Design you
Rule you
Tell you who to be
Listen to your feelings
Follow your intuitions
Answer the callings
Of the dreams
You must chase
Individuality
Is yours
Don't ever let
Someone hold
Your paintbrush

Those with eyes
So quick to judge
To make assumptions
On what's seen
There lies more
To what we see
What is seen
Has layers unseen
The unseen
Can be seen
By certain feeling
Attained by knowledge
Of the seen
Within the unseen
Grows faith
The deep emotions
The eye cannot see
Appearance is a lie
For the truth
Is hidden for us
To greatly care
To dive deep
And see more
Than what is seen
To discover
The unseen

Selfish desires
The common aspect
Of humankind
As if giving
Without getting
Is so terrible
The hungry thought
Of how to benefit
From sacrifice
Instead of relinquishing
Contentedly letting go
Of some attachment
The green value
Kept hidden
And secure
As if more precious
Than the people
Claimed dear
Value never mattered
The lives do
The blessings do
Time is more
Never material things
For one day
They shall perish
And satisfaction
Not achieved
For to be content
One must believe
Less is more
Giving is greater
Receiving the joy
Of smiles
Full hearts
Overflowing love
Never the objects
(cont.)

But the people
The experiences
Feeling whole
Is detaching
From things
And soaking in
Pools of gratitude
With arms wide open
Saying "here is everything I have"
Now naked shall be
Clothed in thankfulness

Chug the bottles
Ease the pain
Smoke the plant
Ease the stress
Take the shots
Escape the world
Swallow the pills
Ignore the hurt
Eat the food
Feel the comfort
Skip the meals
Take the control
Shout the words
Release the anger
Silence the mouth
Stuff the emotions
Beat the body
Feel the strength
Feed the thoughts
Enjoy the madness
And suddenly
Addictions
Inhuman
Dead

Quite a cause for spite
As I witness
Rivers of blood
Stream out of me
Like a punishment
And I wonder
In utter complaint
Why women must suffer
Every single month
With such a ferocious beast
Feeling like we'd rather die
Than have excruciating stabs
Repeatedly in the gut
Ought it unfair
The horrendous predicament
One has most of her life
When the consort is at ease
Allowed to keep his ichor
For all the cruel misery
Of numerous emotions
And repugnant sickness
A woman must cope with
Might be the cause
Of why she hates
Her permanently
Uncorked body

Somehow the madness branches
Like a tree sprouting
From the skull
High into the sky
Where it stands alone
Proud to be different
To be the odd
The unique
The peculiar
Roots planted in chaos
All for the sake of art
To express freely
The voices in the mind
Finally being released
Into the clouds
The wind
Let the crazy out

I eat sugar
Not caring of the consequences
Diabetes doesn't exist
The taste of sweets
Happens to be my high
I crave chocolate
Like an addictive drug
To ease my pain
To alleviate my sorrow
And I think
That if I died tomorrow
I would regret not partaking in
The pleasurable sensation
Of sugar for my buds
When I do die
After eating the misery away
Chewing to find a speck of joy
It will be because
I drowned in white powder
Let it devour every part of me
Karma
I ate too much
Sugar

We like the sting
The burn in the swallow
The lustrous appeal
Of swigging liquor
The common man
The stereotypical alcoholic
Just as much of pirates
Drinking to ease the emotions
A bottle for pain
A jug for misery
A pitcher for sadness
A flask for cheer
A taste so lovely
Yet so corruptive
But we freely voyage
Into the horizon
Anchored to the addiction
Obsessed with alcohol
As the source of treasure

The first time you left
Seeking more money
Leaving behind true love
And shattering a heart
Blinded by greed
You carelessly fled
And to think you were done
But the habits continued
You gold digger
Selfish in pursuit
To consume high amount
Letting go of morals
Forgetting what matters
Corrupted you are
Falling foolishly into the arms
Of a swank life
To keep a rich person
All just to leave
When their pockets are empty
And you're no longer spoiled
You hypocrite
Acting like you care
Pretending you are pure
When in reality
You swim in a pool
Of dirty deeds
Thinking you won't drown
Believing you won't sink
But soon the waters will roar
The lies will suffocate you
The pride will feed on you
And your greed will kill you
In the name of money
Will you rot away in hell
Surrounded by flames
Of your own doing
(cont.)

Since you chose
Dollars over everything
You created the idol
Of eternal misery
Wait until it happens
When Karma comes
To wreak havoc on you
Like you did to everyone else

From behind the bars
I wept in regret
Of decisions made
Feeling self-hatred
Course through my veins
Like a burning wildfire
But amidst the anger
A small stream of pleasure
Pooled off of rebellion
And the invigorating notion
To break the rules
That I allowed to happen
Resurfaced within prison
Such an ignorant mind
Full of stupid choices
Now a captive
With a taste of liberation
But chained to the actions
For the rest of time

I am a woman
Boxed into stereotypes
Like the rest of them
If I didn't shave
Would I be disgusting
If I kept a bare face
Would I be ugly
If I uncross my legs
Am I a sex toy
When I wear shorts
Am I a slut
If my pants are snug
Am I a whore
And excuse me for being
More successful than a man
I bust my ass while he sits
Ought I a maid in his eyes
And excuse me for showing
More confidence than a man
I sweat while he drinks
Ought I a barbie in his eyes
Am I a game in his eyes
Am I a test car
For him to drive
And leave behind
Am I of any value
The world has shaped
What a woman is
And now women have told
The world and the men
Who women are
We are humans
With feelings
With rights
We are strong
And we can do
(cont.)

We can be
We can achieve
Anything that men can
And we have broken
Through the chains
Of stereotypes
So men
Respect us
Someday
You might have a daughter

No longer did I want to carry
These fragile bones
I wished them to break
From malnourishment
Starving to death
Rotting away in self misery
Not seeing a purpose to live
Done with breathing
As much as eating
Swallowing for control
Stress consumed my brain
Until nothing was left
Only dark compelling voices
Whispering lies of escape
"Don't feed the flesh you hate
Let it wilt away to dust"
For dust is all I am
And so shall I return
Not to be mourned
Nor miss the horrific world
And its corruptive diseases
Which spread like hives
So that I rip and tear at my skin
Trapped in this broken body
Prisoner to the demons
That cursed me
With anorexia

Seen as peculiar
But I smile
Wearing it like a crown
Or a glorious robe
Eccentric is my honor
Mysterious is my sentiment
So please continue
To stare in disapproval
Make me an outcast
Because the truth
Is that I indulge
On doses of abnormality
Finding that uniqueness
Is the perfect fit
And if my style
Does not appeal
I don't care
Nor will I ever
Have a problem
Fuck off

A wildfire dances in his eyes
As smoke coruscates around his face
The rush of exhilaration
Courses through his veins
Seeping into his blood stream
Soaking into the depths of his lungs
Ignited discovery now a tried thrill
He didn't believe it intoxicating
That despised smell on the streets
But once experienced he understood
That aside from the negatives
And threat to his health
The jolt of excitement
Was the overpowering choice
For him to carry a pack or two
To light quite a few
Tobacco always on his breath
But it's better than meth
And it eased his pain
From going dark again

If there is a path
Show it to me
Lead me down it
I don't know
The right direction
Facing the intersection
But I know
What I want
They say it's wrong
I thought it was right
Now I'm lost
In a daze
My mind a maze
Confusion my companion
Would I wake up
If I found the path
Straight and sure
But directions
Still taunt me
I'm left a mess

Electrified senses
Let's raise the roof
Like we're meant to do
Born to light up
This colorful world
Of smoke and smiles
Jamming to tunes
That rock the soul
Burst the eardrums
Tongues out
No guns out
Explode loud
That craziness
Dancing like animals
Of the same breed
Same kind
Hands in the air
Without a care
The rowdy screams
A euphoric song
As bodies shake
The ground quakes
At this party
For the fearless
For the reckless
We're all here
Where's the beer

The scariest thing of all
Making life decisions
Aware that choices
Affect future happenings
Though maybe oblivious
To the consequences
Of certain actions
Either mind's place
Still must decide
And therefore does
What is hopefully right
But doubt creeps in
The fear of failure
Like a toxic gas
Like a caustic poison
One bite from the apple
And fallen
Into the worry

With liquor on his breath
Smoke in his lungs
Tattoos on his skin
He goes a little crazy
With his wild heart
And dauntless spirit
Never a dull moment
Or a bored soul
When he's around
The model of fearless
He'd strip in public
To see your shock
You must've forgotten
He's no dog on a leash
Lion in a cage
Can't be tamed
That guy you claim
You don't like it
He'll tell you
To leave him
He shouldn't have to
Take orders from you
When he's being himself

Write myself to sleep
Shall the words
Be a lullaby
A synchronization
With my reveries
And ripple a peace
So soothing
Brings my mind
To rest
But I still hold
The pencil
The thoughts
Keep me
Awake

My crave for sugar
Stabs like a knife
When happiness hits
Not watching my back
The craving attacks
It sneakily creeps
Lurking in my mind
An evil temptation
To overindulge
To be overpowered
By the weakness
Of sweets

Her smile was seductive
With wine-stained lips
Puckered and spread
Revealing white pearls
The purest teeth
Contradicting to her desires
And enchanting eyes
Like rich chocolate
Lined with black ink
Like the peeking tattoo
On her lower back
So a part of you
Yearns to indulge
To taste the sugar
That cast the spell
Deep within your bones
Arousing your senses
To devalue your morals
Diminish your control
So that you surrender
Satiate the craving
By falling into her trap
And if you get out
She'll leave a scar
So you won't forget
The lustful error

Shamed me
For being a rebel
When I wasn't
So now
You get one
Bold and real

You tried to write
My story as yours
For too many chapters
I let you control
Every aspect of me
But I grew tired
Of being the character
You wanted
Being the chess piece
You maneuvered
Being the player
You manipulated
So I quit
Burnt the pages
Of the past
Took a pen
To blank paper
In a new book
And began to write
My own story
My character of choice
Finally the author
Of my life

What a wretched cliché
You mindlessly believed
Calling her a dumb blonde
That gorgeous girl
You aimlessly criticized
She saw the lethal hurt
In a widowed woman's eyes
And saved her life
By words of comfort
She saw the aching hunger
In a destitute man's frame
And nourished his being
By giving him everything
She saw the empty spirit
In a blind child's soul
And suffused them with joy
By sacrificing her days
That gracious girl
You harshly ridiculed
Has a heart so vast
Yet you failed to notice
Because of the lies
They convinced you of
Do not judge appearance
Without knowing the core

Cold metal digs
Into my wrists
And all I feel
Is shame
The mistake made
Replays over and over
Reliving the moment
That once was thrilling
Now an act of stupidity
I'd felt controlled
And the urge
To break completely free
Overpowered my sense
I rebelled
So here I am
As a criminal
More trapped
Than before
Handcuffed

You speak constantly
Letting words flow
Like an ongoing stream
Never thinking
Just saying
And feeling
For yourself
Instead of listening
Caring for others
Opening your heart
To accept love
You use words
Meaningless speech
To fill the void
So empty
Your talk
Is plenty

On the verge
Of something great
Can almost taste it
Feel it within reach
But impatience
Is toxic
The yearning
Is ferocious
Unable to rest
Wanting so badly
Clinging to slight hope
Maybe soon
Obtaining the prize
Until then
Waiting is torture
Wishing is brutal
Dreaming is mockery
Teased by the sight
Of the reality
What could be
Isn't yet
Present

Spiraling down
The dark tunnel
Of reckless behavior
Seeking attention
Never given
The younger days
Spent ignored
Trying to please
The careless souls
That sparked the mayhem
To a sadistic mind
Acts of destruction
Crying for affection
But insanity
Pushed away humanity
Alone in madness
Created by the loss
Of former hope
If the adulation
For damage
And poison
Doesn't kill you
Your mind will

Those rich little bastards
Crying over the dead dog
On their flat screen
But ignoring the destitute soul
Begging for a drink
Beside their mansion
While it storms he waits
But funny fools never cared
Probably made him invisible
While they sit and eat
In luxurious dining
Dressed in lavish clothes
Their neighbor in rags
Skipping meals for his dog
Still the poor man
Never envies the wealthy
Because they don't understand
The simple blessings
The tiny pleasures
He wakes up everyday
And smiles
Grateful to be alive

Every day I awake
And go to war
With myself
Fighting battles
Throughout the day
Trying to live
In the light
But tempted
Strained
Lured
Succumbed
By the forces
Of evil
Around me
Within me
I want to fight
Resisting the appeal
But wanting to taste
Holding back
But wanting to break
Strength weakens
And I slip
Unsure
If I'll stand
Ever again

Dying would be easier
Than coping
The voices say
Give up on life
Too much worrying
Too much caring
Always disappointment
But deciding
To let go
Of the stressors
Made the thoughts
Of ending the journey
Disappear
Happiness appeared

Corruptive behavior
Not wanted
But caused
Because they critique
Put down
Criticize
Every little thing
Never able to please
No matter
The sacrifices
The time
Striving for approval
That will never come
They wrecked you
Your spirit
Your dreams
All of you destroyed
Because they manipulate
Tear apart
Control
Every little thing

She is flattering
In that dress
With that smile
And kind demeanor
She appears elegant
So you'd never guess
Her disguise
But honestly
She's got a sailor's mouth
And body art you can't see
She's multi-layered
But she hides
The best sides

There are too many
Thoughts and voices
Swirling around
Clouding vision
Blocking senses
Controlling me
Taking me captive
Into the vortex
Of mayhem
And the only way
To fight
Against the madness
Poetry
As my shield

Losing you
Was so traumatic
That I never wanted
To love again
The pit in my stomach
Barely able to breathe
Blinded by tears
Choking on screams
As your name is printed
On a grave
As your body is placed
In a casket
I protested
Against the fact
That you were gone
And the rest of my time
I won't be able
To stare into your eyes
To study your face
To feel your touch
The pain I feel
Is so overwhelming
That I wish
To be buried
With you
Because you were
My whole world
And without you
I am nothing
But an empty void

My stoner friend
I finally understand you
Life got too painful
The anxiety too unbearable
The despair too intolerable
So you masked the suffering
By a psychedelic escape
Away from the emotions
You turn to the plant
Your favorite addiction
To distort reality
Into a fantasy
You wanted lasting happiness
And a better life
But don't you know
The smoke drifts astray
The feeling fades away
And it's still up to you
To choose
To see the magic
In your life
Without looking through
The warped vision
Of smoking pot

Forever wondering why
The questions needing answers
Are never justified
Because "they" hide
The secretive truth
From those who see
And hear the lies
They speak of
All for control
For what they believe
As structure
But their words
Contort views
To captivate followers
Align opinions
Enslave the minds
Of those gullible
Closed boxed fools
Who don't even wonder
Why "they" is in charge
When "they" is without
The slightest name
Or a caring soul

It feels like a pill
Lodged in your throat
A pain that won't disappear
No matter how many times
You swallow again
Scratching at your skin
Ripping flesh from bone
As the pain burns stronger
As the despair attacks deeper
The lump in your throat
Now a dagger
Penetrating every organ
Halting every breath
So that the only sound
Is the blood dripping
Pooling around you
Until all that's left
Is red floor
Pale corpse
Empty of the sorrow
Because of the end
Emotions and thoughts
Are the most dangerous
Because they kill
From the inside out

Trying to please you
Had me spinning
In circles of frustration
No matter how hard
I tried to perform
The greatest show
I never received
The applause I sought
And soon I realized
You were never
Worth my time
That if I were
To ever be appreciated
It would be
By the standards
Of my own gig
The orchestration
Of my own choices
Instead of aiming
For your approval
I lived to please
The one off stage
The one who knows
That identity
Doesn't require a disguise
Or someone else's role
The one proud
To be themselves
Without ever needing
A standing ovation
The one who learned
That to be happy
In their own skin
Meant never reaching
The expectations
And being better off
(cont.)

Joyful and independent
Than disappointed and alone
I discovered
That pleasing people
Was more lonesome
Than living for myself
So when I quit
The fake performance
It was as if
The whole world
Was cheering my name
At the moment
Of my victory
Deciding not to care
What other people think

Growing up alone
Accustomed to the lack
Of friends that lasted
Self-reliance evolved
And independence
Was solely known
Until one day
Surrounded by love
By smiles and laughter
Times for memories
Remained a while
So realizing
The need for people
Is a strong crave
Meant that when
The silence came again
It was dreadful
Far too lonesome
Much too boring
But surprisingly
Silence became
The biggest fear
Even though
It used to be
The best friend
There is always
Change
And you can't
Trust completely
Watch your back
But don't be alone
For too long

Never believe the lies
It's not about being enough
Not flattering enough
Not smart enough
Not strong enough
Not brave enough
Not successful enough
There is no such thing
Just be you
Be proud of that truth
You are perfect
Just the way you are
Own it
The world is better
With a unique you
Than the dullness
Of enough

That little child
Always happy
A smile from ear to ear
Those innocent eyes
That carefree spirit
Not a worry for the day
Just living and breathing
Without a question for life
The purpose or meaning
Are words unknown
Lost for hours in magic
With vivid imagination
No cry for escape
No attachment to reality
A new world created
For fun fantasies
That child knew how
To live in contentment
No matter where
No matter the situation
That child knew how
To dance in the rain
I'd love to find her again
I'd love to be her again

They adore the technology
The progression of overstimulation
The ability to sit long
Staring at the screens
Instead of experiencing
The natural world
They don't like to think
Not anymore
They want a machine
To do it for them
They don't want to talk
They want a device
To speak for them
They don't want to go out
They want a service
To bring things to them
They threw the books away
They shut the doors
Blocking out the sunlight
Never seeing the trees
Or another human
Face to face
The real forms
Gone to the screens
And they claim
To love freedom
But they are controlled
Ruled by
Technology
A trap they chose
To fall into

The more
I listen to jazz
The more
The poet within me
Comes to life
Moving and grooving
Are the words
Pen to paper
A melodic tempo
In my ears
On my lips
So that I am
Wholly the poems
And the music
Unified into
Electric art
May it continue
To course
Through my veins
And flow outside
My dwelling
To share
The magic
With them

They mock the poet
The only one willing
To tell the truth
Through resolute words
He reveals the depths
The rawness of humanity
The pure and evil sides
That shape the essence
Of an individual
He uncovers the masks
Invisible to the eye
And provides the insight
To see what's real
The genuine feelings
The actual condition
Of people and life itself
But they don't approve
They don't like honesty
Because they were comfortable
Behind the façade
That he dissected
Through experience and observation
He poured out everything
Into explicit discernment
Peeling back the layers
They pretend to ignore
He traveled far
Down the rare path
Searching for consequential lucidity
For the sake of rescuing
The majority already structured
To conceal their raw behavior
He presented the truth
Without a cost
Not wavered by the discrimination
For once they received
(cont.)

Something unbound to a sycophant
Yet they discarded
The sacred words of verity
And condemned the poet a fool
Though he is the wisest
Of them all
May his words
Reign on

www.ingramcontent.com/pod-product-compliance
Lightning Source LLC
Chambersburg PA
CBHW020414080526
44584CB00014B/1320